THE SECOND MOUSE EATS

The Space Between Innovation, Early Adoption, and Success

Mark Donnelly, PhD.

RPSS PUBLISHING - BUFFALO, NEW YORK

drmaddog@hotmail.com

The Second Mouse Eats

Perfect Bound ISBN:978-1-956688-77-1

Printed in the United States of America

10 9 8 7 6 5 4 3 2 1

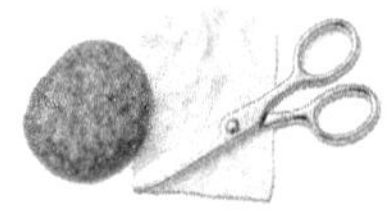

RPSS Publishing - Buffalo, New York

For the first mouse:

For your courage, your curiosity,
and your willingness to test the trap
so the rest of us could understand it.

And for the second mouse:

For your patience, your timing,
and your quiet wisdom in knowing
when to step forward.

We need both.

But this one is for those
who learned, sometimes the hard way,
that survival has its advantages.

Table of Contents

Introduction:
The Trap, the Cheese, and the Applause

There's a story people like to tell about success.

It usually starts with someone being first. First to market. First to discover. First to take the leap while everyone else stood around checking the weather.

We celebrate that person. We build myths around them. We point to their courage as if it were a universal instruction manual.

"Be bold," we say.

"Move fast."

"Get there before anyone else."

It sounds good. It just isn't the whole story.

There's another story. Quieter. Less glamorous. A little harder to turn into a conference keynote.

It involves a mousetrap.

The first mouse sees the cheese and charges. Maybe out of hunger. Maybe out of confidence. Maybe because no one told him how this particular arrangement of wood and wire tends to resolve itself.

The trap snaps. The cheese remains.

And then, after a moment that doesn't make the highlight reel, the second mouse steps forward and eats.

No applause. No headlines. Just a full stomach and a continued existence.

This book is about the second mouse.

Not as a joke. Not as a punchline. As a strategy.

Because in a world that worships speed, there is a quiet, stubborn advantage in timing. And timing rarely gets the credit it deserves.

We are living in an age that rewards novelty.

Every week brings a new product, a new platform, a new promise that this–this one right here–changes everything.

Some of them do.Most of them don't. But they all arrive wrapped in the same language:

Revolutionary.

Disruptive.

Game-changing.

And if you're not careful, you start to believe that being early is the same as being smart. It isn't.

Being early means you are absorbing uncertainty.

Sometimes that uncertainty pays off. Sometimes it just absorbs you.

The first mouse matters.

Let's be clear about that.

Without early adopters, without the people willing to step into the unknown, ideas don't move forward. Nothing gets tested. Nothing improves. Nothing gains traction.

They take risks the rest of us benefit from.

They discover what works–and, more importantly, what doesn't.

They are essential.

They are also expensive.

Expensive in money, in time, in frustration, and occasionally in reputation. They pay the "early adopter tax," a premium for things that are unfinished, unrefined, and often unproven.

And then, once the dust settles, once the bugs are fixed and the systems stabilize, everyone else arrives to a much smoother experience.

That's not unfair. That's the process.

The problem isn't that early adopters exist.

The problem is that we misunderstand their role.

We treat them as the model.

We assume that what works for them will work for everyone.

We build products, strategies, and expectations around people who are, by definition, not typical. And then we're surprised when the majority doesn't follow.

The truth is simpler, and a little less flattering:

Most people are not trying to be first. They are trying to be right.

They want something that works. Something reliable. Something that fits into their lives without requiring a complete overhaul of how they think, act, or operate.

They are not chasing novelty. They are solving problems.

This book is about understanding that difference.

It's about recognizing where an idea sits in its lifecycle, and what that means for the people interacting with it.

It's about learning when to move quickly and when to wait. When to experiment and when to observe. When to be the first mouse… and when to let someone else test the trap.

You'll meet the cast of characters along the way.

The innovators who build before the blueprint is finished.

The early adopters who believe before the evidence is complete.

The majority who arrive when the dust settles and the value is clear.

And the holdouts who remind us that not everything new is necessary.

You'll see how ideas actually spread. Not in straight lines, but in uneven waves of curiosity, hesitation, and eventual acceptance.

You'll see why some brilliant ideas fail, while others–less impressive on paper–quietly take over the world. And you'll learn how to navigate all of it without losing your footing.

This is not a book about playing it safe.

It's not an argument for sitting on the sidelines while the world moves forward. It's about playing it smart. Because there's a difference between courage and timing.

One gets the spotlight. The other gets the result.

So the next time you hear someone say, "This changes everything," pause for a moment.

Look at the trap.

Watch who goes first.

And remember: The second mouse eats.

PART I:

THE PEOPLE AT THE EDGE

Chapter 1:
Meet the Cast of Characters

Every new idea enters the world like a stranger at a party.

Some people rush over immediately.

Some watch from across the room.

Some pretend not to notice.

And a few quietly leave early because they liked things better before the music changed.

Welcome to the adoption curve. It's less a theory and more a recurring human comedy.

The Innovators (2.5%) – *The Tinkerers and Troublemakers*

These are the people who don't wait for permission. They build their own version before the official one exists. If a product says "Do Not Open," they've already opened it, modified it, and posted instructions online.

They are fearless, well-funded, or occasionally both. Failure doesn't discourage them. It just gives them something to fix.

They are not normal. And that's fine, because they aren't supposed to be.

The Early Adopters (13.5%) – *The Evangelists with Receipts*

This is where things get interesting.

Early adopters are not just curious. They are influential. They don't just use new things, they talk about them. They explain them. They justify them. They defend them in conversations that did not need to become debates.

They are the bridge between invention and acceptance.

They are also, let's be clear, a little more tolerant than the average human being.

They will overlook missing features.

They will work around obvious flaws.

They will describe inconveniences as "part of the experience."

They are the reason a product gets a second chance.

The Early Majority (34%) – *The Practical Crowd*

This group does not care about your vision. They care if it works.

They will not buy version 1. They might not even buy version 2. But once something becomes stable, useful, and reasonably priced, they step in.

This is where success actually begins.

Up until this point, you have a story. Now you need a product.

The Late Majority (34%) – *The Skeptics*

These folks are not impressed by hype.

They are persuaded by inevitability.

When something becomes so common that avoiding it becomes inconvenient, they reluctantly step forward. Not because they want to, but because the world has moved on without asking them.

The Laggards (16%) – *The Loyal Holdouts*

They are not wrong. Let's get that out of the way.

Laggards are the people who stick with what works. They don't chase trends, and they don't see the point in fixing things that aren't broken.

Sometimes, they are the only ones who avoid a very expensive mistake.

The Twist Nobody Talks About

Here's the part that keeps this from being neat and tidy:

You are not one of these people. You are all of them.

You might be an innovator with technology, a laggard with fashion, an early adopter with books, and part of the late majority when it comes to anything involving passwords.

We move along this curve depending on what we care about, what we understand, and how much nonsense we're willing to tolerate that week.

That's the real story.

Chapter 2:

The Early Adopter Personality

(Visionary or Volunteer Test Dummy?)

Early adopters are often described in glowing terms.

Visionary. Influential. Forward-thinking.

All true.

But there's another description that doesn't make the brochure:

They are professional tolerators of inconvenience.

Let's break this down.

They See What Others Don't–Yet

Early adopters have a particular kind of eyesight.

They can look at something incomplete and imagine what it will become. Where others see flaws, they see potential. Where others see confusion, they see a learning curve.

This is not delusion. It's pattern recognition mixed with optimism.

They've seen enough things evolve that they trust the process.

They Have Social Capital to Spend

Early adopters tend to have a bit of cushion.

Financially, socially, intellectually.

They can afford to be wrong once in a while. They can absorb the cost of a bad purchase or a failed experiment. More importantly, they can risk their reputation by recommending something new.

That last part matters.

Because when an early adopter says, "This is worth your time," people listen.

They Are Comfortable with Imperfection

This is where things get dangerous.

Early adopters are not bothered by rough edges the way most people are. They will troubleshoot, adapt, and improvise. They treat flaws as temporary. The majority does not.

What an early adopter calls "a minor issue," the rest of the world calls "a reason to return it."

They Like Being First *(Even If They Won't Admit It)*

There is a quiet satisfaction in being ahead of the curve. Owning something before it becomes common. Understanding something before it becomes obvious.

It's not always about showing off. But it's not not about showing off either. Prestige is part of the equation, whether acknowledged or not.

So Which Is It? Visionary or Test Dummy?

Both. That's the answer nobody likes because it refuses to flatter.

Early adopters are essential to progress. They move ideas forward, refine them, and give them a chance to survive. They are also the ones who discover what doesn't work… the hard way.

They are the tip of the spear. And the tip of the spear takes the hit first.

Chapter 3:

The Early Adopter Tax

(Paid in Dollars and Dignity)

There is no official line item for it. No receipt.

No checkbox at checkout that says, "Yes, I understand I am overpaying for something unfinished."

But it exists. It is called the early adopter tax. And it comes due every time you decide you cannot wait.

The Price Premium

New technology is expensive. Not because it is better, but because it is new.

Early adopters pay more. That's the deal. They fund the development, the refinement, and eventually the discounts that everyone else enjoys.

Later buyers get better versions for less money. Early adopters get… bragging rights and a firmware update.

The Bug Phase

Version 1 is where reality meets ambition.

Things break. Features don't work as advertised. Instructions assume knowledge that no one actually has. Early adopters become unofficial support staff.

They troubleshoot.

They report issues.

They explain things to others.

Sometimes they even convince themselves it's fun.

The Obsolescence Trap

This one stings.

You invest early. You commit. You adapt. And then version 2 arrives.

It's better. It's cheaper. It fixes everything you worked around.

Suddenly, your cutting-edge device feels like a historical artifact.

You weren't wrong. You were just early.

The Emotional Cost

This is the part nobody measures.

> The frustration of things not working.
>
> The time spent figuring them out.
>
> The quiet realization that you paid more for less.

And yet…

Most early adopters will do it again.

Because the upside–the moment when something does work, when it changes how you think or operate–is worth the risk.

At least, that's what they tell themselves. And sometimes, they're right.

PART II:
The Promise & the Problem

CHAPTER 4:

The Good

(Why We Need These Brave Souls)

Every system needs its advance scouts.

Not the ones with perfect maps and tidy plans. The other kind. The ones who head out before the road exists, step into the mud, and come back with stories that are half-warning, half-invitation.

That's your early adopter.

Without them, innovation doesn't stall dramatically. It just… sits. Like a car idling in neutral, engine humming, going nowhere.

They Turn Possibility into Proof

An idea is fragile until someone actually uses it.

You can build a prototype. You can craft a pitch. You can dress it up in language so polished it practically winks. But until someone takes out their wallet and says, "I'll try it," it's still just a well-dressed maybe.

Early adopters make the first leap. They take something theoretical and give it a pulse. They test it in the wild where variables don't behave and users don't read instructions. They reveal what works, what breaks, and what should have been obvious in hindsight.

They turn "could be" into "has been." That's a powerful shift.

They Provide Feedback You Can't Fake

Surveys are polite. Early adopters are not.

They will tell you what works, what doesn't, and what made them mutter under their breath at 11:30 on a Tuesday night. They don't just report bugs. They narrate their experience. And that experience is gold.

Not because it's always correct, but because it's real. It's lived. It's messy in all the ways your product will eventually encounter when it leaves the safety of your imagination.

Their feedback shapes the next version whether you like it or not.

Ignore it, and you're building in a vacuum. Listen too closely, and you'll build something only they can love.

There's an art to knowing the difference.

They Create Momentum When None Exists

Markets don't move because of logic. They move because of belief.

Early adopters supply the first spark of that belief. They talk about what they're using. They demonstrate it. They answer questions from people who weren't even curious five minutes ago.

They make the unfamiliar slightly less strange.

And slowly, almost reluctantly, others begin to lean in.

"Wait… what is that?"

"Does it actually work?"

"Would I use something like that?"

That's momentum.

It doesn't arrive with a drumroll. It builds through small conversations, repeated exposure, and a growing sense that maybe this thing isn't going away.

They Become Your Lighthouse Customers

Every new idea needs a visible success story.

Someone who uses it well. Someone others can point to and say, "See? It works for them." Early adopters often become that example.

Not because they're perfect, but because they're first. They figure things out early, adapt quickly, and create use cases you didn't anticipate.

They become proof by existence. And in markets full of skepticism, proof beats persuasion every time.

They Carry the Weight of Uncertainty

Here's the part that rarely gets acknowledged:

Early adopters absorb risk on behalf of everyone else.

They deal with the incomplete versions, the uncertain outcomes, the missing infrastructure. They operate without a safety net and without the benefit of hindsight.

They take the hit first. Which is precisely why they matter.

Because once they've done it, once they've shown it can be done, the rest of the world feels a little safer stepping forward.

Chapter 5:

The Bad

(When the Feedback Goes Sideways)

Early adopters are helpful. They are also, in very specific ways, completely untrustworthy.

Not intentionally. Not maliciously. But structurally, predictably, and with great enthusiasm.

If you treat their feedback like gospel, you will build something elegant, powerful… and utterly confusing to most of humanity.

Let's talk about why.

They Are Not Normal Users

This is the first and most important truth. Early adopters are outliers.

They are more patient.

More curious.

More willing to tinker.

They will click the thing. Then click it again. Then open a forum, read three threads, and figure out how to make it work.

The average user will click it once. If it doesn't behave, they're done.

So when an early adopter says, "It's easy once you get used to it," what they mean is, I invested time that most people will not.

That's not the same thing.

They Underreport Friction

Early adopters have a peculiar habit. They normalize inconvenience.

A complicated setup becomes "a bit of a process."

A missing feature becomes "coming soon."

A workaround becomes "part of the workflow."

They smooth over rough edges in their own minds because they are invested in the outcome. They want the product to succeed, so they subconsciously help it along.

This is admirable. It is also misleading. Because the majority will not extend the same generosity.

They Are Price-Insensitive *(Which Sounds Great Until It Isn't)*

Early adopters will pay. Not recklessly, but willingly.

They understand that new things cost more. They accept the premium as part of being early. In some cases, the higher price even reinforces the perception of value.

But here's the trap:

What they are willing to pay is not what everyone else is willing to pay. If you base your pricing strategy on early adopters, you may discover–too late–that your real market expects something very different.

Enthusiasm can mask resistance. And resistance tends to show up right after you've committed.

They Give You the Answers You Want to Hear

Not because they're dishonest. Because they're excited.

Early adopters often believe in the idea as much as you do. Sometimes more. They see the potential, and they want to be part of its success story.

So their feedback leans positive.

They highlight what works. They downplay what doesn't. They frame issues as temporary rather than structural.

It feels like validation. But it can also be confirmation bias dressed in optimism.

They Can Pull You Off Course

Here's where things get risky.

If you listen too closely, you start building for them. You add features they request. You optimize for their workflows. You refine the product to match their expectations. And slowly, almost invisibly, you drift.

Away from the broader market.

Away from simplicity.

Away from the people who will eventually determine whether this thing succeeds or fades.

You end up with a product that power users adore and everyone else avoids.

It's a beautiful, intricate machine with no audience.

The Translation Guide

When an early adopter says:

- "It's flexible" = It's complicated
- "It's powerful" = It requires effort
- "It just takes some getting used to"= Most people won't use it

Learn to translate.

It will save you time, money, and a long walk back from the edge.

Chapter 6:

The Ugly

(When Early Success Lies to You)

Nothing is more dangerous than early success.

Not failure. Failure is loud, immediate, and instructive. It tells you something is wrong and demands attention.

Early success whispers. It tells you everything is working. And if you're not careful, you'll believe it.

The Conversion Mirage

Early adopters convert at high rates.

They sign up. They buy. They engage. They move through your carefully designed funnel like it was built specifically for them. Because, in a way, it was.

They are motivated. Curious. Willing to explore.

So your numbers look good. Better than expected, even. You start to think:

"We've got something here." And you do.

Just not necessarily what you think. Because when the next group arrives, the early majority, the numbers change.

They hesitate.

They question.

They drop off.

Suddenly, your conversion rates look less like a victory and more like a memory.

The Retention Illusion

Early adopters stick around.

They invest time in learning the system. They build habits. They incorporate the product into their routines.

They stay. Which creates the impression of strong retention.

But their loyalty is not purely functional. It's emotional. They enjoy being part of something new. They derive value from exploration itself.

The majority does not. They stay only if it works consistently, simply, and without friction. So when retention dips later, it feels like something broke.

Often, nothing broke. You just reached a different audience.

The Product-Market Fit Mirage

This is the big one.

Early traction feels like validation.

People are using the product. They're talking about it. They're recommending it. The energy is real, and it's contagious.

It looks like product-market fit. But it might be product-early-adopter fit. And those are not the same thing.

One sustains a business. The other starts one.

Confusing the two is how promising ideas stall right when they should be accelerating.

The Feedback Loop That Tightens Instead of Expands

As early adopters engage, they give feedback.

You respond. You improve. They engage more.

It feels like progress.But if all that feedback comes from the same type of user, the loop becomes closed.

You refine the product for a narrow audience.

You optimize within a bubble. And when new users arrive, they don't see refinement. They see complexity.

The Moment of Reckoning

Eventually, every product faces it.

The moment when it leaves the comfort of early adopters and meets the broader world. This is where the story changes.

The questions shift:

- "Is this interesting?" becomes "Is this useful?"
- "Can it do this?" becomes "Is it easy?"
- "Is it new?" becomes "Is it worth it?"

And if you've built something that only works for the first group, this is where it shows.

Not dramatically. Not all at once. Just enough to slow things down.And in markets that move quickly, slowing down is often the beginning of being left behind.

The Only Way Through

You don't avoid early adopters. You need them.

But you don't mistake them for the destination.

They are the beginning of the journey.

Not the map.

Not the road.

And certainly not the entire landscape.

PART III: Crossing into the Real World

Chapter 7:
The Diffusion Curve
(How Ideas Actually Spread -Slowly, Then Suddenly)

If you've ever watched a pot of water come to a boil, you already understand innovation.

Nothing happens.

Nothing happens.

A bubble.

Nothing happens.

Then suddenly, the whole thing is alive. That's the diffusion curve.

Not a straight line. Not a steady climb. More like a long stretch of patience followed by a rush that makes everyone forget how long they waited.

The Shape of Human Hesitation

On paper, the curve looks elegant. A smooth rise from innovators to early adopters, through the majority, and finally to the holdouts who arrive just in time for the sequel.

In reality, it feels like pushing a reluctant boulder uphill.

Early on, progress is slow because the audience is small. You're speaking to people who already like new things. They don't need much convincing.

Then you hit the middle. And the middle is where ideas go to prove themselves.

Why the Middle Matters More Than the Beginning

The early stages get attention. They're exciting. They feel like momentum. People are talking. Numbers are moving. But they are not the market.

The real test begins when you leave the comfort of early adopters and face the early majority. This group is not impressed by novelty. They are persuaded by utility.

They don't ask, "What is this?"

They ask, "Why would I use it?"

And if your answer requires enthusiasm instead of clarity, you're in trouble.

The Slow Burn Before the Surge

Most ideas spend far longer in the early stages than anyone expects. Founders grow restless. Marketers get creative. Investors start asking questions that come with polite smiles and sharp edges.

"Why isn't this growing faster?"

"Who else is using it?"

"What's the plan to scale?"

The answer, more often than anyone likes, is time.

Adoption is not just about awareness. It's about trust. And trust builds slowly, through repetition, visibility, and the quiet accumulation of proof. You cannot rush it without breaking something.

The Moment It Tips

Then something changes. Not dramatically. Not with a headline.

Just enough people have adopted the idea that it starts to feel… normal.

You hear about it twice in one week. Then three times. Someone you trust mentions it. You see it in use, not as a novelty, but as a tool.

The question shifts from "Should I?" to "Why haven't I?"

That's the tipping point. It's not magic. It's momentum finally catching up with belief.

Most people overestimate how quickly adoption happens.

They also underestimate how completely it happens once it starts.

Ideas don't trickle into the mainstream. They linger, then they arrive all at once like they've been there the whole time.

Chapter 8:

The Five Stages of Adoption

(A Courtship Story)

Adoption is often described like a process.Linear. Predictable. Step-by-step.

That's tidy.

Reality is closer to a relationship. Messy, hesitant, occasionally irrational, and full of second thoughts.

Let's walk through it the way it actually unfolds.

Stage 1: Awareness – "What is this thing?"

This is the first encounter. You hear about something new. A product, a service, an idea. It drifts into your awareness without asking permission.

At this stage, you don't care.

Not because you're dismissive, but because you're busy. The world is full of new things, and most of them don't matter to you.

Awareness is not interest. It's just the door opening.

Stage 2: Interest – "Tell me more…"

Something catches. Maybe it solves a problem you recognize. Maybe someone you trust mentions it. Maybe it simply shows up enough times that ignoring it becomes inconvenient.

You lean in. You read. You watch. You ask questions.

This is curiosity, not commitment. A lot of ideas lose people right here by being either too vague or too complicated.

If you can't explain it simply, you won't get past this stage.

Stage 3: Evaluation – "Will this ruin my life?"

This is where things get serious.

You weigh the idea. Not in abstract terms, but in practical ones.

- How hard is this to learn?
- What does it replace?
- What happens if it doesn't work?

You are not looking for perfection. You are looking for reassurance.

And this is where early adopters quietly step onto the stage again. Their experiences, their stories, their visible use of the product–they reduce uncertainty.

They don't eliminate risk. They make it feel manageable.

Stage 4: Trial – "Let's see if it explodes"

Now you test.

Carefully.

You don't go all in. You try a small version. A limited use. A cautious step. You're watching for friction.

Does it behave the way you expect? Does it integrate into your routine, or does it demand a complete rewrite of how you operate?

This is where many ideas falter. Not because they're bad, but because they ask too much, too soon.

Stage 5: Adoption – "Fine, I'm in"

This is the quiet commitment.

You stop thinking of it as "new" and start treating it as normal.

It becomes part of your routine. You recommend it without hesitation. You forget what it was like before it existed. And that's the goal.

Not excitement. Integration.

The Part Nobody Mentions

You can exit at any stage.

Lose interest. Reject the idea. Try it and walk away.

Adoption is not guaranteed. It's earned. And every step along the way is an opportunity to lose someone who was almost convinced.

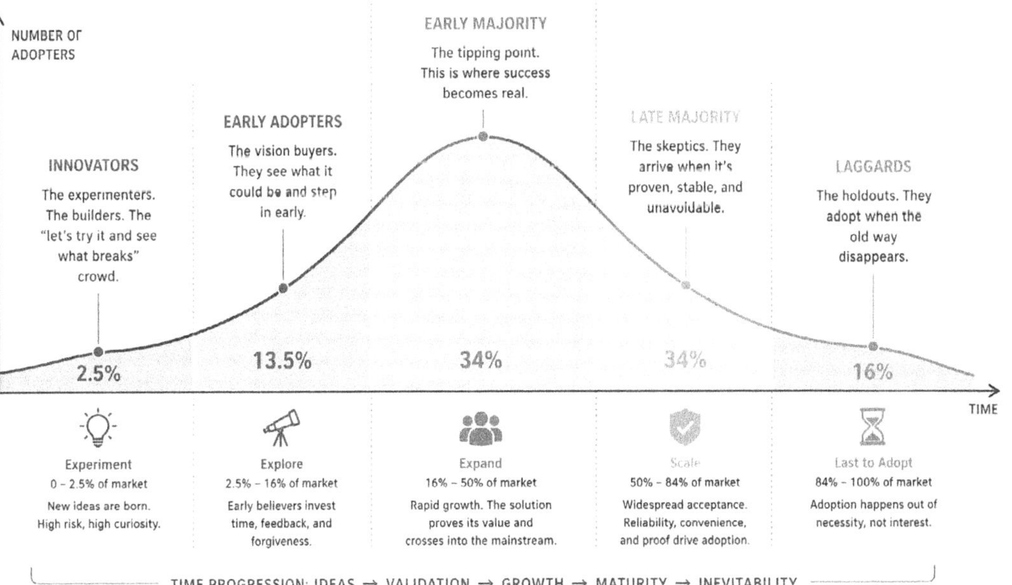

CHAPTER 9:

Marketing to Early Adopters Without Sounding Like a Sales Brochure

Early adopters do not respond well to traditional marketing.

You can throw features at them. You can polish your messaging until it shines. You can list benefits in tidy bullet points.

They will nod politely. And then ignore you. Because early adopters are not looking for polish. They are looking for potential.

Sell the Future, Not the Feature List

Early adopters are motivated by what something could become.

They don't need a finished story. They want a compelling direction.

Where is this going?

What does it unlock?

Why does it matter?

Give Them Something to Do, Not Just Something to Buy

Early adopters like participation.

They want access, insight, influence. Invite them in.

Let them test. Let them provide feedback. Let them feel like part of the process, not just recipients of the outcome.

This is not manipulation. It's alignment.

They want to shape the future. You need help shaping the product. That's a partnership, whether you call it that or not.

Be Honest About the Imperfections

This one surprises people. You do not need to pretend everything is perfect. In fact, you shouldn't.

Early adopters expect rough edges. They're suspicious of anything that appears too polished, too complete, too finished.

Tell them what works.

Tell them what doesn't.

Tell them what you're working on.

You'll earn more trust with honesty than you ever will with perfection.

Tell a Story Worth Repeating

Early adopters talk. That's part of their role.

They explain things to others. They recommend. They demonstrate.

Give them something worth repeating. Not just facts, but a narrative.

Why this exists. What problem it solves. What makes it different.

If they can't explain it easily, they won't. And if they don't talk about it, your momentum stalls before it starts.

A Reminder

Marketing to early adopters is not about persuasion. It's about resonance.

You're not convincing them to care. You're showing them something they already want to care about.

Do that well, and they'll do the rest for you.

Do it poorly, and you'll be talking to yourself.

Chapter 10:

UTAUT

Why People Say "I'll Think About It" … and Then Don't

There's a quiet moment in every innovation's life.

The demo is over. The excitement fades. The pitch has been made. And someone leans back and says:

"I'll think about it."

That sentence has stopped more innovations than bad engineering ever has.

Enter the Unified Theory of Acceptance and Use of Technology, a framework built to answer one deceptively simple question:

Why do people actually use new technology… or not?

The Core Idea: Intention Drives Behavior

At the heart of UTAUT is a simple premise:

People don't use technology because it exists. They use it because they intend to use it. And that intention is shaped by a handful of very human considerations–not technical specs, not marketing slogans, but practical judgments about value, effort, and social pressure.

As the model explains, actual use is driven by behavioral intention, which is influenced by four key factors :

- Performance Expectancy
- Effort Expectancy
- Social Influence
- Facilitating Conditions

Think of these as the four quiet voices in someone's head when they're deciding whether to adopt something new.

The Four Forces *(The Real Decision-Makers)*

1. Performance Expectancy: "Will This Actually Help Me?"

This is the heavyweight. Performance expectancy is the belief that using the technology will improve outcomes–make work faster, easier, better.

If people don't see a clear benefit, nothing else matters. You can have the sleekest interface in the world. If it doesn't solve a real problem, adoption stalls.

This is consistently the strongest predictor of intention .

If it doesn't help, it doesn't happen.

2. Effort Expectancy: "How Hard Is This Going to Be?"

Now we get practical.

Even if something is useful, people hesitate if it looks complicated. Effort expectancy is about ease of use.

Can I figure this out quickly?

Will I need instructions?

Will this ruin my afternoon?

Interestingly, this factor matters most early on–and fades over time as people gain experience.

If it feels like work, people treat it like work… and avoid it.

3. Social Influence: "What Will People Think If I Use This?"

We like to believe we're independent thinkers. We are… until we're not. Social influence captures the effect of others' opinions:

- "Everyone at work is using this."
- "My boss expects me to."
- "People like me are doing this."

This factor becomes especially powerful in mandatory environments, where adoption is driven as much by compliance as by preference .If everyone else is doing it, resistance gets lonely.

4. Facilitating Conditions: "Do I Have What I Need to Make This Work?"

This is the infrastructure question.

Do I have the tools? The support?The system that allows this to function smoothly?

Even if people want to adopt something, they won't if the environment doesn't support it. And over time, this factor shifts from influencing intention to directly affecting actual use .

Even a good idea needs a place to plug in.

The Hidden Variables: Why Not Everyone Thinks the Same

UTAUT doesn't assume everyone reacts the same way.

It recognizes that adoption depends on who you are. Four moderating factors shape how strongly those core drivers matter:

- Age
- Gender
- Experience
- Voluntariness of use

These variables don't change the model. They change the weight of each factor.

A seasoned user may care less about effort.

A new user may care about nothing else.

A mandated system amplifies social influence.

A voluntary one relies more on perceived value.

Why UTAUT Matters (Beyond the Theory)

UTAUT isn't just academic.It explains something every innovator eventually learns the hard way:

Adoption is not about the technology. It's about the user.

You can build something brilliant. But if:

- People don't see the benefit
    - It feels too complicated
    - No one around them is using it
    - Or, the system doesn't support it …it won't spread.

UTAUT2: When Consumers Enter the Picture

The original model focused on organizations. But people behave differently when they're spending their own money.

So along came UTAUT2, adding three new forces:

- Hedonic Motivation *(Is it enjoyable?)*
- Price Value *(Is it worth the cost?)*
- Habit *(Does it become automatic?)*

This version acknowledges something important:

Consumers don't just ask, "Does this work?" They ask:

- "Do I like it?"
- "Can I afford it?"
- "Will I keep using it without thinking?"

Where This Fits in Our Story

UTAUT explains the gap you've seen throughout this book.

Why early adopters jump in while others hesitate.

Why something can be technically sound but commercially weak.

Why some innovations take off–and others stall in that quiet moment of "I'll think about it.

The Synthesis

Every adoption decision comes down to a simple internal checklist:

- Does this help me?
- Is it easy?
- Are others using it?
- Can I actually make it work?

If the answer to all four is "yes," adoption follows. If even one is shaky, hesitation creeps in.

Final Thought

You can build the future. You can market it, explain it, even demonstrate it. But until people believe it fits into their lives–easily, usefully, and without unnecessary friction:

They won't adopt it. They'll think about it. And as any graybeard will tell you… That's where most ideas quietly wait.

Forever.

Chapter 11:

Building for Everyone, Selling to Each

An Inventor's Field Guide to the Adoption Curve

If you want to understand innovation from the outside, watch the customer.

If you want to understand it from the inside, watch the inventor pacing the shop floor at 2:17 a.m., arguing with a prototype that refuses to behave.

Because here's the part most books skip:

Inventors don't build one product. They build several versions of the same idea, each meant for a different kind of person, arriving at a different moment, with a different tolerance for imperfection.

And if they get that sequence wrong, the market doesn't correct them. It ignores them.

The First Decision: Who Is This For–Right Now?

Before anything ships, there's a quiet, strategic choice:

Not "Who will eventually use this?" But "Who can live with this today?"

That answer determines everything:

- How polished the product needs to be
- What features matter
- How it's priced
- How it's explained
- And most importantly... who you talk to first

Because each segment on the adoption curve is not just a different customer.

It's a different expectation of reality.

Stage 1: Building for Innovators *(The Workshop Crowd)*

These are the people who don't need instructions. They prefer not to have them.

What Inventors Build

- Functional prototypes
- Advanced features over polish
- Open systems, flexible, sometimes messy

What They Tolerate

- Bugs
- Missing documentation
- Occasional existential confusion

How It's Marketed

Not really marketed. Shared.

Discussed in forums. Demonstrated in corners of conferences. Passed around like something slightly dangerous but interesting.

Language sounds like:

- "We're experimenting with…"
- "This might break, but…"
- "Here's what we're trying…"

The Goal

Feedback, not scale.

You're not selling a finished product. You're recruiting co-conspirators.

(If your innovators aren't breaking things, you built something too safe.)

Stage 2: Selling to Early Adopters *(The Vision Buyers)*

Now the product starts to look like something.

Not finished.But promising.

What Inventors Build

- A usable version
- Core value clearly demonstrated
- Enough stability to function reliably… most of the time

What They Tolerate

- Rough edges
- Occasional frustration
- Explanations that begin with "In the next update…"

How It's Marketed

This is where storytelling enters.

You're no longer selling a prototype. You're selling a direction.

Language shifts to:

- "Be part of what's next"
- "Get in early"
- "See where this is going"

Pricing Strategy

Premium. Not because it's finished–but because access has value.

The Critical Move

You don't just show what it is. You show what it will become.Early adopters don't buy products. They buy trajectories.

Stage 3: Crossing to the Early Majority *(The Reality Check)*

This is where things get serious. Because now you're no longer selling to believers. You're selling to skeptics with budgets.

What Inventors Must Change

Everything that was "good enough" is no longer enough.

- Interfaces must be intuitive
- Instructions must exist
- Reliability must be consistent
- Support must be real

What They Demand

- Proof
- Case studies
- Demonstrated value

How It's Marketed

No more promises. Now it's:

- "Here's what it does"
- "Here's who's using it"
- "Here's the result"

Language becomes practical.

Measured. Almost boring.

The Hard Truth

Many products die here. Because what impressed early adopters does not satisfy the majority.

The gap between "interesting" and "useful" is where innovation goes to stall.

If your customer needs imagination to understand your product, you're not ready for the majority.

Stage 4: The Late Majority *(The Reluctant Converts)*

By now, your product is no longer new.

It's established.

Which is exactly why this group shows up.

What Inventors Must Deliver

- Stability
- Simplicity
- Compatibility with existing habits

What They Expect

- Low risk
- Clear instructions
- Minimal disruption

How It's Marketed

Reassurance replaces excitement.

- "Trusted by..."
- "Industry standard"
- "Proven and reliable"

Pricing often drops. Bundles appear. Adoption becomes easier than avoidance.

The Real Strategy

You're not convincing them. You're removing their last reason to resist. The late majority doesn't adopt because they're impressed.

They adopt because not adopting becomes inconvenient.

Stage 5: Laggards *(The Final Holdouts)*

These are not your enemies. They are your final exam.

What Inventors Must Accept

You are not selling innovation anymore. You are replacing necessity.

What They Require

- Absolute simplicity
- Familiarity
- A clear reason they must switch

How It's Marketed

Often, it isn't. Change happens because:

- Old systems disappear
- Support ends
- Alternatives vanish

The Quiet Reality

Laggards don't adopt your product. They outlive the old one.

If a laggard adopts your product willingly, check for a miracle.

The Manufacturing Balancing Act

Here's the part that keeps people up at night:

You are not just building a product. You are managing a moving target.

- Too early = not ready
- Too late = irrelevant
- Too complex = abandoned
- Too simple = ignored

Every version is a negotiation between:

What's possible. What's usable And what people are willing to tolerate right now

The Marketing Shift (Across the Curve)

Watch how the message evolves:

Stage	Message
Innovators	"Try this"
Early Adopters	"Be part of this"
Early Majority	"This works"
Late Majority	"Everyone uses this"
Laggards	"You need this now"

Same product. Different conversation.

The Final Lesson

Inventors often fall in love with the first version. Manufacturers fall in love with scale. But success lives somewhere in between.

In the timing. In the transition. In the ability to recognize that the product you launched is not the product that will win.

Final Thought from the Factory Floor

The first version proves you can build it.

The second proves you can improve it.

The third is where people start to trust it.

And somewhere along the way…You stop selling an idea and start delivering something people no longer question.

That's when you've made it across the curve.

And that's when the second mouse shows up…

…not to test anything–

but to eat.

PART IV:

Influence, Momentum, and Missteps

CHAPTER 12

The Tesla Lesson

(Or, How to Sell Risk as Status)

There was a time, not long ago, when buying an electric car required a certain kind of personality.

Not just wealth. Not just curiosity. Conviction.

You were buying into an idea before the world was ready for it. Charging stations were scarce. Range anxiety was a real, daily calculation. The technology was improving, but not yet proven at scale. And still, people lined up.

That wasn't an accident.

The Product Wasn't Just a Car

When Tesla entered the market, it didn't just offer transportation. It offered a narrative.

A break from the past. A bet on the future. A statement that said, "I'm not waiting for this to become normal."

Early adopters didn't just buy the vehicle. They bought the story. And in doing so, they became part of it.

Infrastructure Came Later

This is the part that would terrify a conventional planner. The supporting system wasn't fully built. Charging networks were limited. Service systems were still evolving. The broader ecosystem lagged behind the product itself.

In most industries, that's a fatal flaw. Here, it became a test of belief.

Early adopters accepted the inconvenience because they believed the world would catch up. They planned routes around charging. They adapted their habits. They tolerated friction because they were invested in the outcome.

They weren't just customers. They were participants in a transition.

Prestige Wrapped in Uncertainty

Owning one of those early vehicles carried a certain weight. Not just financial, but social.

It signaled something. Awareness. Forward-thinking. A willingness to step outside the norm. And that matters more than most people admit.

Early adopters are not immune to status. They simply express it differently. Instead of luxury for its own sake, they gravitate toward meaning. Being early becomes a form of identity.

Risk Reframed as Leadership

From the outside, it looked risky. High price. Limited infrastructure. Unproven longevity.

From the inside, it felt like leadership. That shift in perception is everything.

If risk feels like recklessness, adoption stalls. If risk feels like participation in something larger, adoption accelerates.

That's the lesson. You don't eliminate risk. You give it context.

What Made It Work

It wasn't just the product. It was the alignment of three things:

- A clear vision of the future
- A group willing to believe in it early
- A visible path, however imperfect, toward that future

Early adopters didn't need guarantees. They needed direction.

The Takeaway

Most companies try to remove friction before they launch. Some succeed by launching before friction is removed.

The difference is belief.

If people believe the future you're pointing toward is real, they will tolerate the present. If they don't, no amount of polish will save you.

Chapter 13:

The iPhone

A Brick That Became a Pocket Universe

There are products that arrive fully formed.

And then there are products that arrive with just enough brilliance to make you forgive what's missing.

The iPhone belonged firmly in the second category.

The Day the Screen Replaced the World

When the first iPhone was introduced in 2007, it felt less like a phone and more like a magic trick.

A slab of glass. No keyboard. No stylus. Just your fingers, moving things around like you owned the place.

People didn't just watch the demo. They leaned forward.

Because for the first time, interacting with a device didn't feel like operating machinery. It felt… natural.

That was the hook. Not the specs. Not the features. The feeling.

What It Didn't Do *(And What Early Adopters Ignored Anyway)*

Now, let's take the shine off for a moment.

The first iPhone was missing things people took for granted:

- No App Store
- No copy-and-paste
- Slow data speeds
- Limited customization
- Carrier restrictions

By today's standards, it was barely a starter kit. But early adopters didn't see a list of missing features.

They saw a platform waiting to happen.

They were willing to trade completeness for possibility.

The Price Drop Heard Around the World

Then came the moment every early adopter remembers, even if they pretend not to. A few months after launch, Apple cut the price by $200. Overnight.

People who had proudly paid full price suddenly found themselves subsidizing everyone who came after.

There was outrage. Blog posts. Forum threads with the emotional tone of a minor betrayal. Apple eventually offered store credit to ease the sting.

But the lesson stuck: Being first is expensive. Not just in dollars, but in timing.

Why They Stayed Anyway

Here's where it gets interesting. Despite the missing features. Despite the price drop. Despite the rough edges…

Early adopters didn't walk away. Because something underneath all those imperfections was unmistakable. Direction.

The iPhone wasn't finished. But it was right.

The Moment Everything Clicked

Then came the shift. In 2008, Apple launched the App Store.

And suddenly, the iPhone stopped being a product. It became an ecosystem.

Developers flooded in. New uses appeared overnight. The device expanded in ways Apple itself hadn't fully defined.

A phone became:

- A map
- A music studio
- A game console
- A business tool
- A camera people actually used

The early adopters had bet on potential.

Now the rest of the world could see it.

Crossing the Line Into the Majority

At this point, the early majority stepped in. Not because they were impressed by innovation. Because the iPhone had become useful.

Reliable. Expandable. Understandable.

The questions changed:

From: "What is this thing?"

To: "Why don't I have one?"

That's when adoption accelerates. Not when something is new. When something becomes obvious.

The Second Mouse Arrives

By the time later buyers entered the market, they got something very different from what early adopters experienced.

They got:

- A lower price
- More features
- A stable ecosystem
- Fewer frustrations

They didn't need imagination. They had proof.

The second mouse doesn't test the trap. The second mouse gets the cheese.

What the iPhone Teaches Us

The iPhone story is not about technology. It's about timing.

Early adopters:

- Saw the future
- Paid for the privilege
- Lived through the imperfections

The majority:

- Waited
- Watched
- Adopted when the value was undeniable

Both played a role. But they experienced entirely different products.

The Takeaway

Version one is a promise.

Version two is a correction.

Version three is where things start to make sense.

The iPhone didn't win because it was perfect at launch. It won because it improved fast enough for the rest of the world to catch up.

Final Thought

If you had bought the first iPhone, you would have been early.

If you waited a year, you would have been smarter.

If you waited two, you would have been comfortable. And if you waited five, you would have wondered how you ever lived without it.

That's the curve.

That's the pattern. And that's why the story of the iPhone isn't about being first.

It's about what happens after.

Chapter 14:

The Stampede:

What Happens After the First Mouse Survives

The iPhone didn't just introduce a product. It introduced a problem.

Not for consumers. They were busy pinching, swiping, and discovering that a phone could feel less like a device and more like an extension of their hands.

The problem belonged to everyone else.

Because the moment the iPhone worked–really worked, not perfectly, but convincingly–the rest of the industry had to answer a question it had been avoiding:

What are we now?

Not what we were. Not what we've always done.

What we are… in a world where this thing exists.

The Sound of an Industry Recalculating

You could almost hear it.

Not a crash. Not a collapse. More like a collective intake of breath.

Boardrooms went quiet. Product teams started pulling things apart. Roadmaps that looked solid a month ago suddenly felt like they belonged to a different era. Because the iPhone didn't compete on features.

It changed expectations. And expectations are harder to fight than competitors.

The Fastest Pivot: Android Learns to Touch the Screen

Before the iPhone, Android was headed in a different direction. Keyboard-driven. Business-friendly. A sensible evolution of what already existed.

Then Apple arrived with a slab of glass and no keyboard at all.

Google looked at that, and turned the ship. Hard.

Touchscreen became the center. Apps became the ecosystem. The interface became something you felt, not something you navigated.

Manufacturers like Samsung, HTC, and Motorola picked it up and ran.

Fast. Faster than anyone expected.

Android didn't try to out-iPhone the iPhone.

It did something more practical. It spread. Different devices. Different price points. Different markets.

While Apple refined, Android multiplied.

The Ones Who Hesitated: BlackBerry and the Comfort of Yesterday

Before the iPhone, BlackBerry was not just successful. It was essential.

If you worked in business, you had one. If you didn't, you probably wanted one.

> The keyboard was sacred.
>
> Email was instant.
>
> The system worked.

Then the iPhone showed up without any of that.

No keyboard. No enterprise focus. No obvious reason at first to switch.

BlackBerry did what successful companies often do.

They protected what made them successful.

They doubled down on keyboards. They treated touchscreens like a novelty. They watched the market… and waited.

And while they waited, the definition of a smartphone changed underneath them.

The Giant That Couldn't Turn: Nokia

If BlackBerry was dominant, Nokia was everywhere.

Reliable. Durable. Ubiquitous.

They didn't just sell phones. They defined them.

But the iPhone wasn't a better version of what Nokia made. It was something else entirely.A software-first device in a hardware-first world.

Nokia had scale. They had reach. They had momentum.

What they didn't have was speed in the direction that mattered.

They adjusted. Slowly. Carefully.

By the time the adjustment was complete, the market had already moved on.

The Elegant Late Arrival: Microsoft Tries Again

Microsoft saw the shift. And to their credit, they didn't ignore it.

They built Windows Phone, a system that was clean, different, and thoughtfully designed.

> The interface was fresh.
> The performance was solid.
> The experience made sense.
> There was just one problem.
> No one was building for it.

Developers had already chosen their sides.

iOS and Android had the momentum, the users, the energy.

Windows Phone had design. The market had already decided what mattered more.

The Relentless Iteration: Samsung Watches, Then Moves

While others debated, Samsung did something simpler.

They paid attention.

They didn't need to invent the category. They needed to understand it. Then improve it.

Bigger screens.

Faster updates.

More options at more prices.

While Apple moved deliberately, Samsung moved quickly.

Not recklessly. Relentlessly.

They didn't argue about what the iPhone was. They built alongside it.

And in doing so, they became the most consistent challenger in the space.

The Almost Story: Palm Gets Close

There's always one.

The company that sees the future clearly, and still misses it.

Palm Pre had ideas that felt ahead of its time.

Gesture controls.

True multitasking.

A modern operating system.

On paper, it had a fighting chance.

In reality, it didn't have:

- The ecosystem
- The marketing
- The timing

It arrived with good ideas and not enough momentum. And in a market that was accelerating quickly, "almost" didn't register.

What All of Them Missed *(At First)*

The mistake wasn't technical. It was conceptual.

They thought they were competing with a phone. They weren't.

They were competing with a platform.

A system that improved over time. That expanded through apps. That became more valuable the more people used it.

Devices could be compared. Platforms had to be joined.

By the time that became clear, the race had already separated into leaders and followers.

The Second Mouse Strategy

The iPhone was the first mouse. It took the hit.

- Missing features
- High price
- Unproven model

Everyone else had a choice. Rush forward blindly, or watch carefully.

The winners didn't ignore the iPhone. They studied it. They learned:

- What people loved
- What frustrated them
- What mattered enough to scale

Then they built accordingly.

The second mouse doesn't guess. The second mouse observes.

The Takeaway

Innovation doesn't end when a product launches. That's when it begins. Because the real test is not whether something works. It's whether everyone else adjusts.

Some adapt quickly. Some resist. Some never recover. And the difference rarely comes down to intelligence or resources.

It comes down to timing. And the willingness to admit:

"This changes things."

Final Thought

When the iPhone arrived, it didn't kill its competitors. It revealed them.

It showed who could evolve. Who could pivot. And who was still solving yesterday's problem.

And from that moment on, the question wasn't:

"Is this the future?" It was:

"How long can we afford to wait before acting like it is?"

That's the stampede.

And once it starts…

Standing still is the most dangerous move you can make.

Chapter 12:

Netflix

From Red Envelopes to Invisible Infrastructure

There was a time when watching a movie required planning.

You drove somewhere. You browsed shelves. You hoped the thing you wanted wasn't already gone.
And if you forgot to return it, the late fee arrived with the quiet authority of a parking ticket you couldn't argue.

Then along came Netflix–first with red envelopes, then with something far more disruptive:

The idea that movies should simply… appear.

The First Shift: Convenience in an Envelope

Before streaming, Netflix solved a simpler problem.

No late fees. No driving. A queue you controlled from your couch. It wasn't revolutionary in technology. It was revolutionary in friction.They didn't change what you watched. They changed how much effort it took to watch it. And that was enough to start the shift.

The Second Shift: Streaming *(In Theory)*

In 2007, Netflix introduced streaming.

If you look back now, it's tempting to imagine it landed like a thunderclap. It didn't. It landed like a shrug.

The early version of streaming was… fine.

- Limited content
- Low resolution
- Buffering that felt like a philosophical exercise in patience

Meanwhile, DVDs still arrived in crisp, reliable envelopes. Better quality. More selection. No interruptions. By any practical measure, the old system was superior.

So Why Did Anyone Use It?

Early adopters didn't choose streaming because it was better. They chose it because it was faster.

No waiting.

No planning.

No mailbox.

Just click and play.

Even when the experience wasn't perfect, the direction was obvious. Instant access. That was the bet.

The Majority Watches… and Waits

Most people didn't jump immediately.

They noticed streaming. They tried it once or twice. Then they went back to what worked. Because for the majority, "almost good enough" is still not good enough.

They weren't looking for novelty. They were looking for reliability. And early streaming didn't quite deliver that.

The Infrastructure Catches Up

Then something changed–not all at once, but steadily. Internet speeds improved. Content libraries expanded.

Devices integrated streaming more seamlessly. Smart TVs. Game consoles. Phones.

Streaming stopped being a feature and started becoming a default.

The friction disappeared. And once friction disappears, behavior changes quickly.

The Moment DVDs Became an Afterthought

At some point–quietly, without ceremony–the balance tipped.People stopped asking, "Should I stream this?"

They started asking, "Why would I wait?"

The red envelopes didn't vanish overnight. They just became unnecessary.

The better experience didn't replace the old one. The easier experience did.

The Early Adopter Experience

Let's be clear about what early adopters actually got:

- Inconsistent performance
- Limited options
- A sense of experimentation

They tolerated buffering.

They accepted tradeoffs.

They explained it to others who weren't convinced.

They weren't enjoying the final product.

They were exploring a direction.

The Majority Experience

When the majority arrived, they got something entirely different:

- Reliable playback
- Massive libraries
- Seamless integration into daily life

They didn't have to imagine the future. They were living in it.

The Second Mouse Logs In

The first mouse clicked "play" and waited for the buffer. The second mouse hit "play" and watched the movie.

That's the difference. Same idea. Different timing.

Why Netflix Won

It wasn't because streaming was perfect at launch. It wasn't even because it was better.It was because Netflix understood something fundamental:If you reduce friction enough, behavior will follow.

Not immediately. But inevitably.

The Takeaway

People don't adopt new technology because it's impressive. They adopt it because it's easier. Streaming didn't win because it was revolutionary. It won because, eventually, it became effortless.

Final Thought

If you were early, you endured buffering. If you waited, you got binge-watching. If you waited longer, you forgot there was ever another way.

That's how real change happens. Not in a flash. But in a slow erosion of inconvenience… until the old way simply stops making sense.

Chapter 13:

Google Glass

When the Future Arrived Before We Were Ready

Some ideas fail because they're bad. Others fail because they're early. And then there are the rare few that fail because they are both right… and unwelcome.

Google Glass was one of those ideas.

The Promise: A Screen Without a Screen

When Google introduced Glass in 2013, it looked like something pulled straight from a science fiction storyboard. A lightweight frame. A small display hovering just above your line of sight.

Information layered over reality itself.

No phone in your hand.

No screen in your pocket.

Just glance, and the world answers back.

Navigation. Messages. Photos. Video.

The future wasn't in your palm anymore. It was on your face.

The Early Adopters Step Forward

Google didn't launch Glass quietly. They made it exclusive.

An invite-only program. A $1,500 price tag. A sense that if you had one, you were part of something ahead of its time. And early adopters came. Developers. Technologists. Curious optimists.

They wore Glass in public. In meetings. At cafés. At conferences.

They demonstrated it. Explained it. Defended it.

They weren't just using a product.

They were representing an idea.

What Worked *(Technically Speaking)*

On paper, Glass was impressive. Hands-free access to information.

Voice commands. Real-time capture of photos and video.

It wasn't perfect, but it was functional enough to prove the concept.

The technology was emerging. The direction was clear.

What Didn't Work *(Socially Speaking)*

And then the room got uncomfortable. People noticed the camera.

They noticed it wasn't always obvious when it was recording. They noticed that conversations suddenly felt different. Privacy concerns spread quickly.

Restaurants banned Glass. Bars asked users to leave. The word "Glasshole" entered the vocabulary with surprising speed and very little affection.

The issue wasn't performance. It was presence.

The Unwritten Rules Were Broken

Every technology operates within a set of social expectations.

Phones are visible. Cameras are intentional. Screens are held, not worn. Glass disrupted those expectations without giving people time to adjust.

It introduced ambiguity. Am I being recorded?

Is this person paying attention?

Is this normal?

When people don't have clear answers to those questions, they default to discomfort. And discomfort spreads faster than adoption.

Too Early for the World It Entered

Glass wasn't wrong. Augmented reality is still coming. Still evolving. Still pushing forward. But in 2013, the world wasn't ready to accept it in that form.

The infrastructure wasn't mature.
The design wasn't subtle enough.
The social contract hadn't caught up.

It asked people to change behavior before they understood the benefit. That's a difficult ask.

The Early Adopter Experience

Those who embraced Glass experienced something unique.

They got:

- A glimpse of the future
- Access to a developing platform
- A front-row seat to innovation in progress

They also got:

- Social resistance
- Awkward interactions
- A product that quickly lost mainstream support

They weren't just testing the technology. They were testing society's tolerance for it.

The Quiet Exit

Eventually, Google pulled the consumer version. No dramatic collapse. No single moment of failure. Just a gradual realization:

This wasn't the right time.

Glass didn't disappear entirely. It shifted into enterprise use–manufacturing, healthcare, specialized environments where the benefits outweighed the social friction.

The idea survived. The context changed.

The Lesson That Lingers

Google Glass teaches a different kind of lesson than success stories.

It reminds us that innovation is not just technical. It is cultural.

You can build something that works perfectly… and still fail if people don't want it in their lives.

The Takeaway

The first mouse wore Glass proudly.

The second mouse looked at the room… and decided to wait.

Final Thought

One day, something like Glass will return. Smaller. Smarter. More accepted. And when it does, it will feel inevitable.

People will wonder why it took so long. They won't remember the early adopters who tried it first. But those early adopters will remember. Because they weren't wrong.

They were just early… in a world that wasn't ready to look back at them.

Chapter 14:

Opinion Leaders, Gatekeepers, and the Social Domino Effect

Ideas do not spread evenly. They move through people. And not all people carry the same weight.

Some voices travel further. Some opinions stick longer.

Some individuals act like hinges, quietly swinging entire doors open or closed.

The Myth of Equal Influence

It's comforting to think that everyone has an equal say. In practice, influence is unevenly distributed.

Certain individuals sit at the center of conversations. They are listened to, quoted, referenced. Their approval reduces uncertainty for others.

These are your opinion leaders. They don't always have titles. They don't always seek attention. But when they speak, others lean in.

Why Early Adopters Often Become Opinion Leaders

Early adopters arrive first. That alone gives them an advantage.

They have experience when others have questions. They have stories when others have speculation. They can demonstrate instead of describe. And that creates authority.

Not formal authority. Practical authority.

"Here's how it works."

"Here's what to expect."

"Here's what I'd do differently."

That kind of guidance carries weight.

Gatekeepers: The Quiet Filters

Not all influence is visible. Some people don't amplify ideas. They filter them. They decide what enters a conversation and what gets ignored. They curate information, often without announcing that they're doing it.

These are gatekeepers.

They might be editors, managers, community leaders, or simply the person everyone asks before trying something new.

If they dismiss an idea, it struggles to spread. If they allow it through, it gains a foothold.

The Two-Step Flow *(Or Why Ads Don't Do All the Work)*

Mass messaging has its place. But most people don't act because of a message. They act because someone they trust interprets that message.

First, the idea reaches an opinion leader.

Then, the opinion leader passes it along in a way that feels credible.

That's the domino effect. It doesn't look dramatic. It doesn't make headlines. But it's how adoption actually happens.

Trust Travels Through Familiar Paths

People don't evaluate every new idea from scratch. They rely on shortcuts.

- "Who else is using this?"
- "Do I trust them?"
- "Does this fit what I already know?"

Influence flows along existing relationships. Friends, colleagues, communities.

Ideas don't jump randomly. They move through networks that already exist.

The Risk of Misplaced Influence

Not all opinion leaders represent the broader market.

Some are too advanced. Too technical. Too removed from everyday use.

If they dominate the conversation, they can unintentionally skew perception. They highlight strengths the majority doesn't value. They overlook barriers the majority won't tolerate. And suddenly, the narrative around the product feels… off.

Positive, but disconnected.

A Reminder

You don't need everyone to talk about your idea. You need the right people to talk about it in the right rooms.

Find those people. Respect their role. And remember that influence is less about volume and more about credibility.

Chapter 15:
Networks, Clusters, and the Echo Chamber Problem

Ideas spread like conversations at a long table.

They move from person to person, sometimes quickly, sometimes slowly, shaped by who's sitting where and who's willing to speak up.

But not all tables are the same.

Some are tightly packed, full of familiar faces. Others stretch across rooms, connecting people who don't usually interact. And the difference between those tables determines how far an idea travels.

Clusters: Where Ideas Catch Fire Quickly

A cluster is a group of closely connected people.

Same industry. Same interests. Same conversations.

Within a cluster, ideas move fast. One person adopts. Others notice. Discussions begin. Experiments follow.

Before long, it feels like "everyone" is using the new thing.

But here's the catch: "Everyone" often means everyone in that group.

The Illusion of Widespread Adoption

Inside a cluster, momentum feels larger than it is. You hear about the idea repeatedly. You see it in use. You assume it's gaining traction everywhere.

It isn't. It's gaining traction here.

This creates a dangerous illusion.

You believe the idea has broken into the mainstream when it's still circulating within a relatively small circle.

Weak Ties: The Bridges Between Worlds

If clusters are tight circles, weak ties are the threads that connect them.

A colleague in another department. A friend in a different industry. A casual connection who brings in something unfamiliar.

These connections don't carry the same depth of trust, but they carry something just as important: New information.

They introduce ideas into places where they haven't already been discussed to exhaustion.

Without weak ties, ideas stay local. With them, ideas travel.

The Echo Chamber Problem

When a product lives too long inside a cluster, something subtle happens. Everyone starts agreeing.

Feedback becomes predictable. Perspectives narrow. Assumptions go unchallenged. It feels like alignment. It's actually insulation.

You refine the product based on similar viewpoints. You reinforce what the group already believes. You lose sight of how it appears to outsiders. And when it finally reaches a new audience, the reaction is not what you expected.

Breaking Out of the Bubble

To grow, ideas must leave their original environment.

That means discomfort. Different users. Different expectations. Different levels of patience.

What worked in one cluster may not translate cleanly to another.

But that's the point. Adaptation is how ideas scale.

The Balance Between Focus and Reach

You need clusters. They provide early momentum, concentrated feedback, and a sense of progress. But you also need bridges.

Connections that carry the idea outward, into unfamiliar territory where it can be tested again.

Too much focus, and you stagnate. Too much spread, and you lose coherence. The balance is delicate.

The Observation

If everyone around you agrees that your idea is brilliant, you are either very lucky… or not talking to enough different people.

Probably the second one.

PART V:

Where Good Ideas Struggle

Chapter 16:
The Organizational Version of All This
(Meetings Included)

If individuals adopt ideas like a cautious courtship, organizations adopt them like a family deciding where to go to dinner.

Slowly. Loudly. With at least one person asking a question that was already answered twice.

Innovation inside organizations is not just about the idea. It's about alignment. And alignment is a creature that requires feeding.

The Myth of the Decisive Leader

There's a popular image of innovation in organizations.

A bold leader makes a call. A direction is set. The company moves forward. It happens. Rarely.

Most of the time, adoption is not a single decision. It's a series of small approvals, quiet resistances, and negotiated compromises.

Even when a leader says "yes," the organization still has to figure out how. And that's where things slow down.

Collective Decisions: Consensus with Coffee

In many organizations, adoption is a group effort. Departments weigh in. Stakeholders ask questions. Meetings multiply like rabbits in a favorable climate.

This isn't inefficiency. It's risk management.

Organizations don't just ask, "Does this work?" They ask:

- Will this disrupt existing systems?
- Who needs to be trained?
- What happens if it fails?
- Who gets blamed?

These are not small questions.

They are the difference between a smooth rollout and a long apology.

Authority Decisions: Fast, Then Complicated

Sometimes, a decision is made at the top. "This is the direction."

It sounds efficient. It often is… at first.

But implementation still requires buy-in from the people who actually use the system. If they don't understand it, trust it, or see the value, they will resist.

Quietly, creatively, and with remarkable persistence. The idea may be adopted on paper. In practice, it stalls.

The Champion: The Person Who Refuses to Let It Die

Every successful innovation inside an organization has a champion.

Not always the highest-ranking person. Not always the most visible. But the most persistent.

They answer questions. They address concerns. They keep the idea moving when momentum fades. They are the translator between vision and reality.

Without them, even good ideas lose energy. With them, even difficult ideas have a chance.

Why Organizations Move Slower Than Individuals

An individual can take a risk. An organization absorbs one. That difference matters.

Individuals experiment. Organizations evaluate.

Individuals can pivot quickly. Organizations must consider the cost of changing direction. So they move carefully.

Which feels slow… until you realize the stakes.

The Translation

When an organization says:

- "We're exploring this" = We are not ready
- "We're piloting this" = We are testing it cautiously
- "We're evaluating feedback" = We are deciding whether to proceed

Nothing is ever as fast as it sounds. And nothing is as slow as it feels from the inside.

Chapter 17:
Why Some Brilliant Ideas Fail Anyway

Not every good idea wins. That's the uncomfortable truth.

Some fail quietly. Some fade. Some never make it out of the room they were introduced in. And it's not always because they were flawed.

Sometimes, they were simply… wrong for the moment.

Better Is Not Always Enough

An innovation can be objectively better.

Faster. Cheaper. More efficient. And still fail.

Because "better" is only part of the equation.

People also ask:

- Is it familiar?
- Does it fit what I already do?
- Will it create more work before it saves time?

If the answer to that last question is "yes," adoption slows. Not because people are irrational. Because they are practical.

Timing: The Silent Dealbreaker

Too early is indistinguishable from wrong. An idea can arrive before the infrastructure exists. Before the audience is ready. Before the problem feels urgent enough to solve.

It can sit, waiting. Sometimes it returns later, dressed slightly differently, and succeeds. The idea didn't change much.

The timing did.

Cultural Resistance: The Invisible Wall

Every group has habits. Ways of working. Ways of thinking.

Unspoken rules about what is acceptable and what is not.

An innovation that disrupts those patterns faces resistance. Not always openly. Sometimes it's hesitation. Delay. A quiet preference for the familiar.

This is not ignorance. It's inertia. And inertia is powerful.

Complexity Is the Quiet Killer

The more an idea demands, the harder it is to adopt.

New skills. New systems. New ways of thinking. Each requirement adds friction.

Early adopters may push through. The majority will not.

They are not looking for transformation. They are looking for improvement.

There's a difference.

The Cost of Switching

Every innovation replaces something. Even if what it replaces is imperfect, it is known.

Switching carries risk.

- Time to learn
- Potential mistakes
- Disruption to routine

If the perceived benefit does not clearly outweigh the cost, adoption stalls.

Not because the idea lacks merit. Because the tradeoff isn't obvious enough.

The Verdict

Failure is rarely about a single flaw.

It's usually a combination of small mismatches.

Too early.
Too complex.
Too unfamiliar.
Too demanding.

Stack them together, and even a brilliant idea struggles.

PART VI:

Getting It Right

(Or Less Wrong)

CHAPTER 18:

How to Use Early Adopters Without Letting Them Drive the Bus

Early adopters are valuable. They are also not in charge. That distinction matters more than most people realize.Because if you hand them the wheel, they will drive with confidence… in a direction most people won't follow.

Listen Carefully, Filter Aggressively

Early adopters provide insight.But not all insight is equal.

Some feedback points to real issues. Friction that will affect everyone. Gaps that need to be addressed.

Other feedback reflects preferences. Advanced use cases. Edge scenarios.

Your job is not to accept everything. It's to distinguish between signal and noise.

Segment Your Audience Early

Not all users are the same. Treating them as if they are leads to confusion.

Identify your early adopters. Track their behavior separately.

Understand how they differ from the broader audience. Because when the majority arrives, their needs will not match. And you'll need to adjust.

Measure Behavior, Not Enthusiasm

Early adopters are enthusiastic. They will tell you they love the product. They will recommend it. Discuss it. Defend it.

But enthusiasm is not the same as sustained use.

Watch what people do.

- Do they return?
- Do they complete key actions?
- Do they integrate it into their routine?

Behavior tells the truth. Words sometimes tell a better story.

Build for the Many, Not the Few

This is where discipline comes in. It's tempting to optimize for your most engaged users. They are responsive. Vocal. Appreciative. But they are not the majority.

If your goal is growth, you must simplify. Reduce friction. Clarify value. Make the product accessible without explanation.

What feels like "dumbing it down" is often just making it usable.

Validate Beyond the Inner Circle

At some point, you need to step outside the early adopter group.

Test with new users. People who don't know the backstory. Who haven't invested time. Who approach the product without context.

Their reactions will feel harsher. They will expose weaknesses the early group overlooked. That's not a problem.

That's progress.

The Rule

Early adopters are your scouts.

They go ahead. They report back. But you don't build the entire city based on where the scouts camped for the night.

Chapter 19:
Rules for Surviving Innovation

By now, you've seen the pattern.

Excitement.

Adoption.

Friction.

Adjustment.

Expansion.

It repeats, with variations, across industries and ideas.

So let's close this section with a few rules. Not laws. Not guarantees. Just observations earned the long way.

Rule #1:
If It Requires a Firmware Update to Function, Wait

Early versions are rarely stable.

They improve. Rapidly. Patience is often rewarded with a better product at a lower cost.

Rule #2:
Never Confuse Excitement with Stability

Buzz is loud. Stability is quiet. If something is all excitement and no consistency, it's still in the early stages. Proceed accordingly.

Rule #3:
The Second Version Is Usually the Honest One

Version one is ambition.

Version two is correction.

By the third, you start to see what the product was meant to be all along.

Rule #4:
Simplicity Wins More Often Than Power

Complex systems impress. Simple systems spread.

If people need instructions to get started, adoption slows. If they can figure it out immediately, it grows.

Rule #5:
Timing Matters More Than Brilliance

A good idea at the wrong time struggles.
A decent idea at the right time succeeds.

Pay attention to readiness, not just quality.

Rule #6:
Listen to Early Adopters, But Watch Everyone Else

Feedback is useful. Behavior is decisive. If the majority hesitates, there's a reason.

Find it.

Rule #7:
Progress Is Real, But It's Not Even

Innovation does not move in straight lines.
It pauses. It surges. It doubles back. Expect irregularity.

Plan for it.

Rule #8:
You Don't Have to Be First to Be Right

There is a quiet advantage in arriving later. Seeing what worked. Avoiding what didn't. Building on proven ground.

First is not always best.

Final Thought from the Porch

Every generation believes it is living through unprecedented change. And in some ways, it is.

But the pattern underneath is familiar.

New ideas arrive. A few embrace them.

Most wait.

Eventually, they become normal. Then something else comes along. And the cycle begins again.

The trick is not to chase every new thing.

It's to recognize which juice is worth the squeeze.

Epilogue:

The Long View from the Porch

By the time you've seen a few cycles of innovation come and go, something changes. Not your curiosity. That tends to stick around, stubborn as ever. But your pace.

You stop sprinting toward every new idea like it's handing out free money. You stop dismissing things outright just because they sound unfamiliar. You develop a kind of calibrated patience, the ability to lean forward without falling over.

You learn to watch.

Everything New Becomes Ordinary

There was a time when the things we now take for granted felt improbable.

Electric lights.

Automobiles.

Telephones that didn't require a wall.

Each one arrived with its own chorus of skeptics and believers. Each one passed through the same stages. Early enthusiasm, uneven adoption, gradual acceptance.

And now? They are invisible.

Not because they lack importance, but because they have been fully absorbed into the rhythm of everyday life.

That's the destination of every successful innovation. Not applause. Normalcy.

The Edge Moves, But the Pattern Doesn't

The details change. The names. The technologies. The industries.

But the pattern underneath remains stubbornly consistent.

A small group steps forward first. They experiment, adapt, and report back.

The majority waits, watches, and eventually decides The idea either spreads or fades. And then, without ceremony, the next idea appears.

New edge. Same curve.

Wisdom Is Not Resistance

There's a temptation, as you gain experience, to become dismissive. To see something new and say, "I've seen this before."

Sometimes you have. Sometimes you haven't.

Wisdom isn't about rejecting change. It's about recognizing its shape.

Understanding where something sits on the curve. Knowing when to engage, when to wait, and when to walk away entirely.

That's not cynicism. That's perspective.

Curiosity, Tempered

The goal is not to become a laggard. Nor is it to live permanently on the bleeding edge, collecting first versions like souvenirs. It's to remain curious… with boundaries.

To explore without overcommitting.

To adopt without losing judgment.

To appreciate novelty without being ruled by it.

A kind of balanced curiosity. Not dull. Not reckless.

The Quiet Advantage of Experience

Once you understand the pattern, something interesting happens. You stop reacting. You start anticipating.

You can see when enthusiasm is outpacing reality. When feedback is coming from too narrow a group. When a product is about to leave the early stage and meet its real test.

You don't predict perfectly. No one does.

But you recognize the signs. And that's enough to make better decisions than you used to.

A Final Word

Somewhere, right now, someone is opening a box.

Inside is a product that promises to change something. Maybe something small. Maybe something large.

It smells like fresh paint.

It hums with possibility.

It also contains a few things that don't quite work yet. And the person holding it is smiling anyway.

Because they see what it might become.

That person is an early adopter. They will test it. Talk about it. Help shape it. And in time, the rest of the world will decide what to do with it.

Just like always.

Pull up a chair when you can.

Watch the cycle.

You'll start to see it everywhere.

Bibliography

Foundational Works on Diffusion & Adoption

Rogers, E. M. (2003). *Diffusion of innovations* (5th ed.). Free Press.

(Originally published 1962)

Moore, G. A. (2014). *Crossing the chasm: Marketing and selling high-tech products to mainstream customers* (3rd ed.). Harper Business.

Ryan, B., & Gross, N. C. (1943). *The diffusion of hybrid seed corn in two Iowa communities.* Rural Sociology, 8(1), 15–24.

Technology Adoption & Market Behavior

Loudon, D. L., & Della Bitta, A. J. (1993). *Consumer behavior: Concepts and applications* (4th ed.). McGraw-Hill.

Noel, H. (2009). *Consumer behaviour.* AVA Academia.

Bass, F. M. (1969). . Management Science, 15(5), 215–227.

Innovation Diffusion in Organizations

Strang, D., & Soule, S. A. (1998). *Diffusion in organizations and social movements: From hybrid corn to poison pills.* Annual Review of Sociology, 24, 265–290.

Greenhalgh, T., Robert, G., Macfarlane, F., Bate, P., & Kyriakidou, O. (2004). *Diffusion of innovations in service organizations: Systematic review and recommendations.* Milbank Quarterly, 82(4), 581–629.

Attewell, P. (1992). *Technology diffusion and organizational learning: The case of business computing.* Organization Science, 3(1), 1–19.

Networks, Influence, and Social Systems

Valente, T. W. (1995). *Network models of the diffusion of innovations.* Hampton Press.

Rogers, E. M., & Shoemaker, F. F. (1971). *Communication of innovations: A cross-cultural approach*. Free Press.

McPherson, M., Smith-Lovin, L., & Cook, J. M. (2001). *Birds of a feather: Homophily in social networks.* Annual Review of Sociology, 27, 415–444.

Behavioral Models & Adoption Theory Extensions

Davis, F. D. (1989). *Perceived usefulness, perceived ease of use, and user acceptance of information technology.* MIS Quarterly, 13(3), 319–340. (Technology Acceptance Model – TAM)

Venkatesh, V., Morris, M. G., Davis, G. B., & Davis, F. D. (2003). *User acceptance of information technology: Toward a unified view.* MIS Quarterly, 27(3), 425–478. UTAUT Model)

Innovation, Risk, and Market Dynamics

Abrahamson, E. (1991). *Managerial fads and fashions: The diffusion and rejection of innovations.* Academy of Management Review, 16(3), 586–612.

Peres, R., Muller, E., & Mahajan, V. (2010). I*nnovation diffusion and new product growth models: A critical review and research directions.* International Journal of Research in Marketing, 27(2), 91–106.

Historical and Interdisciplinary Context

Tarde, G. (1903). *The laws of imitation.* Henry Holt & Company.

Katz, E., & Lazarsfeld, P. F. (1955). *Personal influence: The part played by people in the flow of mass communications.* Free Press.

Contemporary Perspectives and Applied Insights

Zinilli, A. (2025). *Elements of network science: Theory, methods and applications in Stata, R and Python.* Springer.

If the scholars gave us the map, experience supplied the weather report. And as any graybeard will tell you, both matter.

About the Author

Mark Donnelly, PhD is the graybeard lecturer who turned a squeaky whiteboard and a well-traveled tweed sport coat into a teaching philosophy.

A former marketing professor, brand consultant, author of more than sixty books, historian, photographer, and creative instigator, he has spent decades making complex ideas feel simple, and making people wonder if it's all that coffee, or if he's naturally this intense.

Dr. Donnelly built his reputation the old-fashioned way: by simplifying the truth. Not the polished, buzzword-heavy version, but the kind that holds up after watching trends rise, fall. With more than thirty years in academia, his work has also moved through newspapers, publishing, consulting, community initiatives, and philanthropic strategy collecting stories, experience, and more old books than any one person needs.

At the center of his work is a single question: how do you make important work visible in a way that invites others to take part in it? That question has shaped his approach across education, communication, and non-profit philanthropy, especially in areas where clarity matters and certainty is rare.

Dr. Donnelly lives and creates in Buffalo with his bride, Princess Laura, surrounded by notebooks and half-finished ideas. His guiding principle remains unchanged:

Make a difference.

This book is his latest attempt to do exactly that.

Other Timeless Books in the Graybeard Lectures Series:

Each stands alone.
Together, they form a unique, common sense curriculum.

Graybeard Lectures: Marketing

Drawn from smudged whiteboards and lived experience, This book cuts through buzzwords and trends to reveal how branding, storytelling, word of mouth, and purpose actually work–by understanding humans first. Warm, humorous, and practical, it's a guide for anyone who wants marketing that makes sense and lasts.

Graybeard Lectures: Branding

Branding is not decoration. It's definition.This book challenges the modern habit of treating brands as visual projects instead of behavioral ones. Logos matter less than promises kept. Consistency matters more than cleverness. Reputation is built slowly and lost quickly.

Graybeard Lectures: Advertising

Advertising doesn't fail because people stopped paying attention. It fails because it forgets how attention works.

This book explores why the most effective advertising aligns with human instincts rather than fighting them. It examines timing, context, repetition, and emotional truth without chasing trends or tactics.

Graybeard Lectures: Market Research

Listening Past The Numbers is a clear-eyed look at why market research often delivers confidence instead of understanding. It challenges the misuse of data, dashboards, and statistics, arguing for research grounded in human behavior, context, and judgment. Rather than offering tools, the book offers a wiser way to think, listen, and decide when the numbers start acting certain.

www.ingramcontent.com/pod-product-compliance
Lightning Source LLC
LaVergne TN
LVHW052338100826
845147LV00020B/1108

* 9 7 8 1 9 5 6 6 8 8 7 7 1 *

1 & 2 Thessalonians Personal Workbook

By Chad Sychtysz

Published by
Spiritbuilding Publishers
9700 Ferry Road, Waynesville, OH 45068

1 & 2 THESSALONIANS
Personal Workbook
By Chad Sychtysz

ISBN: 978-1-964-80550-4

Spiritbuilding
PUBLISHERS

spiritbuilding.com